AIRBNB STORIES

Maja Sotenšek

Airbnb Stories

CONTENT

Airbnb Stories 7

Viki and His Father Ben 11

Luna and Mark 15

Max 18

The Viennese Psychiatrist 21

Gustave 24

Marion and Pierre 26

Andy and Sarah 29

Stephen 31

Dorothy and Sam 33

Meike and Nikki 36

Ralph 38

The Big Norwegian Wedding /

Maarja and Ronne 41

Kiki and his family 44

Magi and Lars 47

Beatrice and Alfio 50

Swedish Girls Are Awesome 52

Svetlana 55

Antalya, Turkey 61

The Siwa Oasis, Egypt 64

Bali, Indonesia 67

Marrakech, Morocco 70

Siena, Italy 73

Apulia, Italy / Gianna and Antonio 77

Suzana 82

Elena and Cosimo 84

Palestine and Israel, Jerusalem 87

Nazareth, Kaled 90

Tiberias, Jon 93

Tel Aviv, Edi and Adi 96

Chioggia, Italy, Laura 99

Tamara 105

Ben 2 108

Ana and Piotr 110

Alice and Ron 113

Windy and Lena 115

About me 117

Airbnb Stories

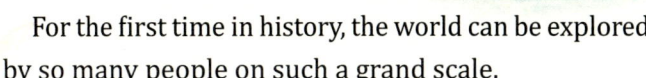

For the first time in history, the world can be explored by so many people on such a grand scale.

Trails that not too long ago were only accessible to merchant caravans, soldiers, sailors or rare adventurers are now open to anyone who has the desire, the will and the courage to explore them.

There is a nomadic spark inside many of us that fans our curiosity to peek outside of our familiar surroundings, see the unknown beauty of the world, take in the foreign atmosphere, the new smells and flavours, get to know different customs, surrender ourselves to unknown challenges and make new friendships.

Airbnb is well-suited to the modern traveller: private but interesting apartments, affordable prices and making new friends is the complete opposite of the boring cookie-cutter hotels with more or less similar furnishings and the expected run-of-the-mill services.

Soon, two years will have passed since I started hosting modern-day vagabonds in my home. I enjoy exploring the world, which is why I like hosting like-minded people.

In the summer, my seaside ground-floor apartment with a small garden is always full of interesting guests from all over the world.

Nowadays, holidays are also different from what they used to be; most people only come for a few days, treating themselves to a short break, just lazing around and swimming in the sea after their mandatory visit to the capital and Bled, and maybe also Bohinj, Postojna Cave or the Škocjan Caves. Very few people visit Slovenia just for the sea.

Our relationships also vary wildly. Sometimes, we can immediately identify a kindred spirit, we instantly click, start chatting and share our stories; on other occasions, we keep our distance and only bump into each other on arrival and departure.

Despite it all, we have amassed quite a few stories together and every single one has enriched me in some way or inspired me with new revelations.

Viki and His Father Ben

Fingers with delicately groomed crimson nails carefully gather the nylon stocking. When they reach the toe cup, the big toe slips into this prepared bed first and is immediately followed by the other toes. Now, the leg effortlessly slips into the precious smooth weave and the young lady diligently smooths out every wrinkle and carefully aligns the vertical seam to accentuate the beauty of her slender legs. She fastens the stocking to the belt with six straps and repeats the process with the other stocking. Finally, she straightens her tight skirt, reaching below her knees, so that it hugs her curves without a single wrinkle. She puts on azure blue cufflinks shaped like forget-me-nots and attaches a matching brooch above her heart. With a few quick strokes, she brushes her hair that she curled with big rollers in the morning and her movie star hair is perfect. She outlines the upper curve of her lip using a bright red lip liner and applies enough lipstick to also spread it across the lower lip with a trained motion. She makes sure that there is no lipstick on her teeth.

A precious little bottle of cologne sits on the dressing table next to the small neo-renaissance mirror. Squeezing the braided pink bulb, she frugally spritzes a little bit of mist on her neck and wrists. When she is ready, she turns and smiles to the man lying on the bed who has been watching her this entire time. How he would enjoy pulling her back under the sheets and continue with their lovemaking, but he cannot bring himself to undo all of her hard work.

Okay, let's go out for dinner! He jumps up off the bed in a single motion; he hastily puts on his trousers, adjusts his shirt and tucks it in, and carelessly puts on his tie – after all, they are on vacation!

They descend the creaky wooden stairs and walk out into the street. A few other couples are already strolling along the seaside and Ben suddenly realises that there is hardly anyone else around apart from the young lovers and a bunch of noisy children.

He takes the hand of his Eve (yes, that is her actual name), puts it over his and pulls her closer. As they playfully stroll down the Punta with sparkles in their eyes, Eve's thin heel gets stuck in the gap between the stone cobbles. Blushing slightly, she manages to skilfully save herself from this little predicament without Ben noticing and gives him a little nudge to the right and onto the asphalt surface, where she can walk more easily.

They are drawn in by the colourful awning of Gostišče Vojko and quickly grab a table that had just freed up. A friendly, plump middle-aged man brings them red wine in stemmed glasses and explains that it is teran, a full-bodied Karst wine rich with iron and minerals. Eve takes a small sip and puts down the glass, and Ben quickly puts his hand on hers. He gazes into her golden brown eyes, which reflect the last rays of the setting sun.

Darling … He clears his throat and tries again. *Darling, let's get married, I want to have you by my side forever!*

He watches her face in slow motion, her refined lines with a narrow aristocratic nose, accentuated cheekbones, small red lips. A curly honey golden lock of hair cheekily bounces against her brow. As he is watching her, he is absolutely convinced that she is the only one he wants to have children with, share a home with, the only one he could watch and admire for all eternity – the way she walks or how she throws her head back when she laughs, how she gently presses against him when she holds onto his arm.

He is suddenly overcome by such warmth that he jumps out of his chair and gets on one knee in front of this beauty that takes his breath away … somewhere on the coast of the Adriatic Sea, in a really small town, in an even smaller restaurant by the sea.

Eve blushes and can hardly hold back the tears as she exclaims *yes, yes, yes …* A jolly man, it turns out to be Vojko, the owner of the place, opens a bottle of sparkling wine and Ben and Eve make a toast together with all the other guests. Out of nowhere, a moustached man with an accordion appears and, before you know it, all the young couples who could be seen strolling along the waterfront earlier start dancing in front of the tables.

Now he is here again, grey-haired Ben and his son Viki. He is sitting where he sat with Eve in 1957 in

Gostišče Vojko. Vojko is long gone and was replaced by a large, loud and soulless pizza place. He does not like it. In his mind, he is constantly talking with Eve; she has merged with him into a single mind and even though her body is gone, Ben feels she is always there with him.

My dear Eve, how I wish Viki would also find a woman like you. Who knows, maybe he will propose to her in Piran too. I brought him here so that we could catch the reflection of our love and inspire him with it. May it give him strength to find his own haven.

 Luna and Mark

The beautiful redhead with luscious curls and porcelain skin brings to memory the dreamy Art Nouveau faces of Alphonse Mucha. A Slovenian with a penchant for art, she has been living in Scotland for a number of years and her Scottish boyfriend with a ruffled, curly head of hair and a mischievous smile looks as though he came straight out of one of Tolkien's tales. Always friendly, smiling and very chatty, he leans towards the listener to reinforce his words, but, unfortunately, I struggle to comprehend what he is saying. His Scottish accent is wonderfully melodic, but difficult to understand to the untrained ear.

We soon discover a shared passion for ancient remains, megalithic circles and menhirs; unusual stone architecture that emits magical energies and inspires people to contemplate their ancient ancestors. Scotland abounds with such ruins, while we have only begun rediscovering them here.

They are among my first *Airbnb* guests, which might be the reason why a special bond forms between us. I am very happy to listen to their suggestions and advice.

They quickly make themselves at home and I like the fact that they always spot the little details in the apartment and make use of them. They light candles in the evening, listen to music and watch the reflection of the moon on the water. Early in the morning, right after sunrise, Mark heads down the coast to the harbour and enthusiastically practices his photography.

We chat every evening and since they have no car here, we sometimes spice up our conversations with short trips around Istria – going for a swim in Alberi, a visit to the flea market in Grožnjan or a stroll down the magical streets of Motovun.

When visiting Grožnjan, a huge round bottle for storing wine or olive oil catches our eye as we are all mesmerised by the fading afternoon light radiating beautifully through the bottle's green glass. Mark heroically puts it on his back and carries it to the car, but it is a whole different story when we have to drag it from the Arze parking garage at top of the hill back to the house. However, the three of us are cut from the same cloth – way too impatient to wait until the morning. We have to see right away where its fragile beauty will be most prominent.

If you ask me, Luna and Mark are so special also because of their relationship, which is always caring and enthusiastic. One time, when the door cracks open for a brief moment and I get a quick behind the scenes look at this perfection, I realise that they leave nothing to chance. They have this agreement that they will consciously control their behaviour: no unnecessary nagging, complaining, or whining, only a lot of caressing, petting, laughing, support and tenderness. This fleeting glimpse, a random and unintentional look, is a precious gift to me and an encouragement for considering how we can delicately develop – or not – our relationships.

It is so easy and, at the same time, so immensely hard; it demands constant vigilance, respect, benevolence, and the constant and careful development of a relationship.

Articulating these rules adds another dimension – the awareness that nurturing love is our choice and responsibility.

MAX

OK, Max it is! If I had a son, this would be his name – I would have named him after a sweet little boy I met at my first job working as a teacher.

This Max, however, came from London. We got on the same page very quickly as we are both interested in travel and history.

In the evening, he mentions that he would like to visit the Škocjan Caves. The tourist office recommended taking a bus to Divača and then continuing on foot.

Surprised by the poor and time-consuming connections, I offer him a ride. I would actually love to go for a walk across the Karst landscape as I have not been in Matavun and its beautiful surrounding area in a while. After a quick tour of Piran the next morning, we huffed and puffed up the Mogoron Hill towards the city walls and the car. Max is writing a doctorate and currently works as a programmer for a famous social network. He loves Slovenia, which is why he has already bought his parents plane tickets to Ljubljana as a gift.

As we are standing on top of the hill, looking over the Piran Peninsula and across the glistening sea to Trieste, the lagoon of Grado and even the silhouette of the Alps, all this incredible beauty seems quite unreal and I can easily image how it can astound a traveller seeing it for the first time and then every time after that as it reveals itself before the amazed person's gaze.

As we arrive to the Škocjan Caves Park, the staff is already getting ready to start the next guided tour. Max joins the group while I set off on a two-hour hike, following the markings of the education trail past Mala and Velika dolina, through the village of Betajna. The walk along the collapse dolines finishes in a picturesque cave with a lake, its silhouette obscured by mist somewhere near the dark opening that leads into the underground. At the end of the trail, I run into Max's group and together we hike back to our starting point.

As we are driving back towards the coast, we can feel the tiredness setting in, partly because of the heat and partly because of the walking. Max's head slumps against the headrest.

It feels so nice touching Beth's hair, so thick, long and wavy.

I brush them by a window covered with a heavy curtain with only a single beam of light streaming through a small opening. I watch as thousands of dust particles reflecting in the light dance around in the golden ray while I cup a lock of hair in my left hand. I bend over to catch the scent of lavender, her favourite oil that she applies a few drops of under her pony tail or on the back of her head every morning. That is when I notice that Beth's body is slowly disintegrating and fading away. I can see tiny atoms rising towards the ceiling in their chaotic dance. Beeeth!!! Beeeth!!!

Max twitches and mumbles. He opens his eyes, frightened. *Where are we?*

We're barely past Divača, I explain hastily. *The town was named after an ancient temple dedicated to Deva, Devača, a female goddess of fertility, like Yoni.*

That maybe it, I just dreamt of a ... goddess ... then she just disappeared, vanished into thin air. Just like real life ... we broke up, my girl and I. It's still hard.

I give him an awkward pat on the shoulder.

Every ending hides the beginning of something new.

Says the ever optimistic Louise Hay, Max chuckles.

THE VIENNESE PSYCHIATRIST

A lady of my age (i. e. late middle age) is dropped off right at my front door by a small electric vehicle, which is a service the town provides free of charge as other motorised vehicles are not allowed in this area. My jaw drops to the floor when I see the mountain of luggage. For a week's stay, she brought not only a suitcase, but also several duffel bags, boxes and sports bags, which take quite some time for her and the friendly driver to unload and stack in front of the door.

Puzzle games, she says with a shrug. Her friends rented an apartment a few houses down the street and they will play them together.

As an advocate of luggage minimalism, I simply cannot comprehend this enormous amount. Surely they did not come to the coast just to play puzzle games?

Ana brought along a large poodle (she described it as a small puppy in our e-correspondence, which is why I reluctantly agreed to go along with it, expecting a chihuahua-sized dog) and while I am showing her around the apartment, she mentions that she intends to use the stove only to heat up the ready-made meals for her dog. *Hmm, a dog mom*, I think to myself with a grain of sarcasm.

The first few days, Ana really does seem to be out a lot, leaving her less-than-happy dog howling behind the locked door. She quickly changes her strategy and starts taking it with her to the beach and to her friends' house, but it does not turn out to be the most well-mannered dog as they have mostly been staying at home and lounging in the garden these past few days.

She calls me one afternoon because of a problem with the stove top. Standing in the kitchen talking, I glance around the apartment and spot a dripping-wet swimsuit. I am surprised she just hung it out to dry on the door handle while she has an entire garden at her disposal. When she notices the look of disbelief and, yes, I have to admit, annoyance on my face, she quickly ends the conversation and ushers me out.

Then, at the end of her stay, comes the shock. All the rooms stink to high heaven of dog poo and despite airing the apartment for several days, cleaning it with all sorts of products and using air fresheners, I cannot get rid of the stench.

I am trying to figure out what had happened. It seems that despite her pedantic mind – or perhaps because of it – Ana had failed to solve the problem of disposing of her dog's poo, which she has been carefully collecting, as a diligent dog owner would, from the pavement and putting it into bags. Just as she felt that drying her swimsuit on the line in the garden, for everyone to see, was unacceptable, she apparently thought it heresy to throw these bags into regular bins, since there are no special bins for dog waste in our little town.

As Mujo and Haso would say in their famous Bosnian jokes: *Some logic, right?*

In order to avoid any future dilemmas of the kind, I went and edited the status on my Airbnb profile the following morning by selecting *NO* next to the *pets allowed* option.

GUSTAVE

As a true Frenchman, he is best described by the words *bon vivant*.

In our e-mail correspondence before his arrival, he did not hide his disgust over the extortionately high prices in both parking garages and I could not help but imagine a person who had been struggling to save up the money for his last-minute vacation in Slovenia.

What should I say? I suggest finding cheaper parking in nearby Lucija, but warn him that it would mean taking a bus to get here.

You can imagine my surprise when a refined gentleman of impeccable manners shows up at my door – yes, he is the headmaster of an *école élémentaire* and his wife is a lawyer. They only came for a short holiday since the *Madame* has an important court proceeding over the weekend that simply could not be postponed. Ah, the parking, they left their car in one of the garages, of course, no problem at all!

I see them every night on the Tartini Square, mesmerized by the classical music concerts, I can hear them playfully making toasts in the evening, drinking fine wine by candlelight and having confidential conversations.

As they are leaving, Gustave, Mr Headmaster, hands me a piece of paper with a list of things he thinks I should buy:
- salad spinner / recommended
- ice bucket / recommended
- ear plugs / suggestion
- better corkscrew / ESSENTIAL!!!
- stemmed champagne glasses / absolutely ESSENTIAL, most important!!!

Ah, the French, I sigh. That salad spinner is more or less just *camouflage*.

Since a lot of my guests this year are French, I eventually do go out to buy those champagne glasses.

À la santé!

Marion and Pierre

They come in quietly, almost invisibly, as if they do not want anyone to notice them. Marion's eyes seem to be constantly in conflict, one watching the person she is talking to and the other fixed on Pierre.

When they are left alone in their room, she carefully fluffs the pillows and helps him to get comfortable on the bed. Pierre takes his old fountain pen, which he always keeps in his wallet, puts his feet up on the footboard, crosses them into his favourite position and starts doing crossword puzzles.

In the meantime, Marion transforms the small kitchen into her battlefield: cooking, chopping, sautéing, roasting, testing flavours and adding spices.

Food is her tool. With it, she brings back Pierre's memories. No, she never really read Proust and she had never heard of the famous passage when a single bite of a *madeleine cake* tears down a dam that releases a liberating river of long-suppressed emotions. Marion, also, is not a psychiatrist, she is but a housewife; however, she tactfully understands the power of flavours and uses them to try and penetrate the wall of her husband's darkness.

As the pot is bubbling and the pleasant smell of her famous *peperonata* fills the room, she takes a moment to glance at her husband. He took a little nap, still holding the magazine firmly, but the pen looks like it could slide through his fingers at any moment. There is a barely-visible smile on his face and Marion is pleased to see him so comfortable.

For a brief moment, she too closes her eyes.

As if in slow motion, Pierre slowly slides towards the floor. She tries to catch him, but he slips from her hands and falls onto the kitchen tiles with the full weight of his body, banging his head against the foot of the table. Flashing lights, siren, hospital. Tears, fear, anxiety. It all spins in front of her eyes in this brief moment in time before she takes a deep breath and steps assuredly back to the stove. She confidently stirs the bubbling dish, drawing spirals into its surface, occasionally giving it a taste with a wooden spoon.

A few minutes later, she is already gently shaking Pierre out of his sleep to invite him to the table. Pierre opens his eyes and gently gazes into hers.

Oh, is it ready? I'm so hungry!

They take a seat at the small apartment table laden with pans, bowls and pots that emit an enticing aroma. *Bon appétit!*

I can't wait to see Celine!

Marion starts at Pierre's remark. It was only this morning that he soullessly shrugged his shoulders when she mentioned Celine, he could not even remember the name of his own daughter. Is her old husband finally back?

Me too! And the twins, we haven't seen them in ages! Truly, darling, I can't wait!

The next morning, as we are saying our goodbyes, I notice an unusual change.

When they had arrived, Pierre did not say a word to me, but now he is cheerful and chatty. He speaks slowly and with difficulty, but you can tell something or someone has set off fireworks in his eyes.

Andy and Sarah

Just a few words about Andy.

Who is the best dad in the world? Andy! Do I really need to explain you what the name of daddy's little princess is? It is Sarah, of course! This is basically all you need to know about Andy and Sarah. They are the best team. Period.

However, daddy's dreams are occasionally invaded by Morana, the goddess of death.

She drags him back under the steely cold of the neon lights where he, just as he did before, keeps getting up off his chair next to the hospital bed, like a jumping jack, trying to hide the sickness by wiping the sweat off her brow. Their time has become a game of Chinese jump rope on the rack of eternity and every second, stretched out to eternity, reduced to a mere drop in the muffled rhythm of the dripping 5-FU chemotherapy medication. It seems completely unreal, science fiction.

He calls for the nurse, she is vomiting into the steel kidney dish and somebody is passing him a roll of paper towels.

He supports her tiny hand in a blue hospital gown, thin and transparent like a breath.

Bald and remote, she keeps breathing, and breathing, and breathing until one morning, when he wakes up and reaches out to her, even the breathing is gone, it died down. It faded away. Disappeared into the blue sky ... just like the magical smoke from Aladdin's lamp.

Just a few weeks ago, his Lena was all smiles as they glided through the park of love in a playful embrace, catching the wind in their unbuttoned trench coats on their way to the kindergarten to pick up their little girl. They went to the amusement park in the afternoon, riding the bumper cars and the swing ride. Up above the people, resembling small toy soldiers, Andy was suddenly struck, in all of its fullness, with the awareness of the happiness he felt of having them, his girls. He reached out to touch them, first Sarah's small hand and then Lena's. They held hands and spun and spun while Pink Floyd's Learning to Fly sounded underneath.

Andy is the best dad. Anyone going through the hosts' reviews on his Airbnb profile can make sure of that.

Every morning, he grabs a brush and parts Sarah's hair, attentively and diligently, into two identical halves in order to weave them into perfect braids.

The girl puts on a frilled skirt adorned with flowers, the kind a Barbie doll would wear; she picked it out herself, of course.

They head to the beach, hand in hand, and stop along the way at a Chinese shop to buy an inflatable ring.

It could have been a perfect day, it almost is, but something is still missing. When they get home, Sarah runs over to me on the balcony for a little cuddle, two strangers who will be saying goodbye to each other soon.

Stephen

Stephen, a young man from Vienna, came to the informatics congress in Portorož to present his project.

As though we had made the arrangement beforehand, I made him an extra-large portion of tomato salad with mozzarella, which turned out to be his only meal that day.

Great, I love that salad! I only have a couple more hours of work, a few corrections. Stephen was already typing away on his laptop at a speed I could only dream of achieving.

The next morning, I got up a bit earlier, but not before him. Once again, he was frantically typing away and nervously going through his papers.

Oh no, there's no internet connection, he moaned after a while. *I can't lose my data*!!!

Come to the second floor, the modem is in this room, I offer. *You can stay here until the evening.*

I leave the house to run some errands. When I come back late in the afternoon, I find Stephen running around the house like a madman, from the ground floor to the second floor, euphorically typing and checking his papers while doing so, all the doors wide open and the curtains wildly fluttering in the wind.

I prepare dinner and invite him to join me. He is grateful, but he wolfs it down in a hurry, completely lost in his own world.

I have to kick him out of the room upstairs at 10 PM and he begrudgingly retires to his apartment.

It somehow becomes natural to me to take care of this youngster. I prepare some breakfast for him in the morning and he is off to the congress.

My favourite Airbnb so far, I have to come back someday with my family for a real vacation!

Come, come, Piran is worth seeing, you don't even know where you've been.

We hug and I wish him luck with his presentation.

Dorothy and Sam

I am sometimes appalled at how full of prejudice I am.

When I see Dorothy and Sam at the door, the first thing that pops into my head is: *My God, they are so old! How did they even survive such a long journey?*

Now, I am ashamed of my reaction. I can even freely admit that they are more energetic, happy and curious, as well as better physically prepared than many people decades younger than them (me, for example).

They came from Australia.

Why Slovenia?

They had heard that we have beautiful mountains. They went on hiking trips in the Soča Valley first and the seaside is their reward.

Great choice! Very few of my guests have heard of the beautiful places in the Soča Valley.

Dorothy and Sam are retired university professors. They have made extensive preparations for the journey and have read hundreds of guide books, internet posts and blogs.

Every year, they go somewhere for a month or two and they have seen quite a bit of the world.

I am honoured, actually, that they have chosen my place.

In the evening, they invite me over for a chat which keeps on going long into the night. Dorothy speaks excellent English, but she speaks quietly and puts emphasis on certain words, so one really has to listen attentively to understand. I can imagine she developed this technique with her students so that they were forced to give her their undivided attention.

Sam is more relaxed and confident.

When they ask me about my work, I mention that I occasionally volunteer at a refugee centre. Sam also has experience in this field of work and he confirms that Australia also has very harsh immigration policies. We find that we are all ashamed of our respective politicians' stances, wire fences and the fact that the bureaucrats who decide the fates of these desperate people have no knowledge of the actual conditions.

Time and again, I have gotten confirmation that people who have visited the places immigrants come from and have experienced their heart and hospitality are capable of showing a lot more compassion.

Would they be interested in me renting bikes for them?

Oh no, definitely not, we're going on a hike along the coast tomorrow, we're going to take a look at everything along the way, Dorothy explains jovially.

Twenty kilometres one way?

Ah, maybe we'll take the bus on the way back.

Did I mention that they are well into their nineties?

After about a month, I was happy to receive a postcard from Castlemaine, Victoria, with a friendly invitation to come and visit them down under at the first opportunity.

Hmm, it will take quite a bit of training before I can even consider visiting them – now that I know that they never sit still.

MEIKE AND NIKKI

Meike is Nikki's mom, they are from Amsterdam. Nikki is in her mid-twenties and she immediately claims the best spot – in the hammock – making herself comfortable there with her mobile phone.

Meike does not look too pleased, but she knows all too well that any negotiation on the matter is a foregone conclusion, so she resigns herself to the old lounge chair – which had already served my grandfather well.

She tries starting a conversation, but Nikki only replies in single syllables. Meike herself is not the most talkative type either, so she quickly gives up and devotes her attention to her own mobile phone.

And so the hourglass sifts the sand of the holidays from one bulb to the other into infinity, as infinite as the messages between Nikki and her friends, and Meike and hers.

I happen to spot them one evening at a seaside bar, each sipping their own Aperol spritz. Sitting comfortably with their feet up on the wall engrossed in their magical screens, they do not notice the screeching seagull nearby, begging for an olive, nor do they notice a group of boys at the next table pulling faces at Nikki.

A few minutes before departure, they quickly put away their mobile phones, throw their belongings into two small suitcases bought specifically for flying budget airlines, give me a quick wave and they are gone.

The next morning, I find a small earring under the bed and I send Meike a text with a photo: *Did one of you lose an earring?*

I don't know, I have to ask Nikki. She's at work now in a different town. I'll speak to her over the weekend. Sure enough, that is when Meike sends me another text: *It's not hers!*

That reminds me that I need to speak with my daughter about something, so I grab my mobile phone to send her a text. I change my mind and call her instead. I want to hear her voice!

RALPH

He impatiently interrupts my monotonous recital of the house rules.

Yes, yes, I know how to use an induction cooker. OK, we will put our information into the notebook.

He rummages feverishly through the refrigerator, preparing a snack. *Should I open the tuna cans?* he shouts to Kemal.

Kemal does not hear him over the water that is running loudly in the bathroom, he is showering and rinsing the sticky sweat from his dark body. He is beautiful, with his short black beard and eyes black like charcoal.

Ralph, all tensed up and hard, is impatient. He opens the bathroom door and draws the shower curtain. Kemal's buttocks are perfect, muscular and bulging. Ralph reaches into the lubricant container with his hand, slips into the bath, turns Kemal around and pushes his upper body slightly downwards.

Kemal closes his eyes and pretends to breathe faster.

Flashing before his eyes are scenes from the epic of the Iraqi people – missile attacks, explosions and projectiles killing people in the bazaar; so inconceivable, like in some alternate reality. A fruitmonger who just moments ago was still spinning a ripe, sumptuous golden melon in his outstretched hand above his head, now has the fruit splattered with the contents from underneath his cranial bone, making him look like an absurd creation of the Maker, a liquefied character from a Dalí painting.

The familiar click of a rusty Kalashnikov when it is ready to fire. He is just a small boy who can barely hold the big rifle with both hands. When he pulls the trigger, the butt of the rifle keeps hitting him in the wound that never heals.

Just like his commander keeps hitting a different wound every night, tearing him apart in pain with short thrusts, over and over again.

The smell of earth ... The smell of earth and smoke coming from the oven, buried a few metres underground, in which his mother is making fresh naan. She is putting the thinly rolled bread onto the hot walls of the oven and singing to herself quietly. Wrapped in a wet cloth, still steaming hot, she spreads them on the ground next to the rice and sauces. The children follow her movements with eyes wide open and full of hunger, waiting for their father to give them permission to take the food.

Kemal breathes heavily and lets out a moan full of longing; *in his mind, he is shuffling his tired legs, all torn up and septic, as he keeps on marching ... he marches across uneven dried mud paths, across fields surrounded by ripe grain, across stone mountain trails where he keeps slipping in his rubber boots, across slushy mud in torrential rain as if the sky had been torn open. He runs from farmers, soldiers, policemen ... He runs in Turkey, Bulgaria, Serbia, Slovenia, Austria.*

Ralph finished a while ago. He is rubbing soap into his body and cleaning him with a sponge, causing soap bubbles to fly into the air.

I am just like this bubble, Kemal realises, *just like a bubble.*

The Big Norwegian Wedding /
Maarja and Ronne

The week that Maarja and Ronne arrived, there was a constant drizzle. True, there were also short sunny spells in between, especially in the mornings, but such bad weather was quite unexpected at the beginning of September.

They arrived full of enthusiasm, euphoria even; a friend who had rented an apartment a few houses down invited them to a proper big Norwegian wedding.

How many of you have flown over from Norway?

About twenty, Ronne explains.

I have to admit I am a little surprised that all the wedding guests came at their own – not so small – expense.

Why Piran? Did they meet here?

Not really, they first met in Venice, but they like Piran better.

It's true, Ronne nods after a short think, *that it's going to be a little tough for them if they'll want to celebrate their wedding anniversary here. Their salaries are not that high.*

Maarja rents a bicycle first thing in the morning and together with the rest of the girls, probably the bridesmaids, they head off to the florist shop in the neighbouring town (our town does not have one).

They come back in a few hours armed with local vines and other local plants which I hope they picked along the way and did not pay a king's ransom for; however, I do notice a few *calla lilies* that are definitely from the florist shop. Maarja starts making the bouquet for the wedding.

She places all the plants on the stone floor and starts arranging them into a nice bouquet.

Congratulations! Are you a florist? I inquire. *No, no, but it'll be fine!* she nods bravely.

I do not know what this bouquet ended up looking like, but the wedding went ahead smoothly.

They made reservations for the wedding reception at a nearby restaurant.

Before they even got to the main meal, the sky went black all of a sudden and a tramontane wind came in with full force. This is the kind of wind that comes out of nowhere and just sweeps away everything in its path. It can easily lift and throw around parasols, blow away tablecloths, break and crack porcelain and glass or anything that one might forget to hide indoors. As I was closing the slamming shutters and scrambling to bring inside all the swimsuits, towels, flower pots and newspapers, I did not even have time to take a peek at how the festive lunch was going.

Shortly thereafter, a wild storm broke loose, it started to absolutely pour down with rain, there was thunder and lightning and the tramontane was replaced by the borra which cooled down the air even further.

Maarja and Ronne came back to their room very soon, before evening, completely soaked, teeth chattering.

To wash away the bitter taste of that divine chastening and the potential consequence of the bad omen, the wedding guests continued toasting long into the night, trying to console the newlyweds.

One could say that their smiles were less than convincing as they were leaving the next morning – let us hope that in the future, the sky will grant the newlyweds more sun!

KIKI AND HIS FAMILY

They came from Singapore. A young family with a five-year-old son.

They reminded me of the different customs, gestures and symbolism in the non-verbal communication of the Chinese, which is sometimes incomprehensible to our way of thinking.

Travelling across this once so distant land, I experienced a lot of funny misunderstandings trying to communicate with gestures – something I did not find problematic in other countries. True, the Chinese do have a perfected system of sign language, but you have to be familiar with it and stick to its conventions. They even use it amongst themselvets in order to communicate with members of other dialect or language groups.

One time when I went to have lunch with my daughter, I ordered one soup and wanted to reinforce that by raising one finger. Unfortunately, it turned out that, according to their sign language, my raised finger only confirmed the waitress' question if she should bring two soups – much to my daughter's dismay who did not fancy it.

Another time, we asked for a sugar-free drink. There were three of us, but none was able to successfully convey *no sugar* with our pantomime skills. The shopkeeper stood there in silence, not seeming to care too much as we ended up desperately waving a bag of sugar in front of her face and exaggeratingly shaking our heads. We could not have been clearer, but obviously not clear enough for her.

It is a land where everything seems to be stretched out between two extremes; on the one hand, you have the limitless poeticism and tenderness and, on the other hand, the uncompromising aggression and ruthlessness. (The Tiananmen Square has a beautiful name, the *Square of Heavenly Peace*, but it is also a place that carries the horrific memory of the student massacre of 1989.)

It was quite a shock for my *European* perception of manners to see young people pushing elders out of the way when fighting for a spot on a public bus. However, this unpleasant experience was immediately erased by the soft sound of the *liuqin*, a Chinese lute we had a chance of hearing in the Chinese Opera. The most soothing music I have ever heard.

As I exchanged a few words with the family in the evening, their little boy had already changed into his comfortable kimono and was lounging on the pillows playing his favourite game on the tablet.

His mother got him to stand up with a few snappy orders. He then placed his hands together into a Buddhist greeting and politely bowed almost all the way to the ground.

I was put on the spot as I did not actually know what kind of bow is appropriate along with the greeting, so I simply bowed my head with my hands in praying position.

The next day, the parents asked me where they could find a Chinese or at least an Asian restaurant nearby. They let out quite a few sighs of disappointment when I explained that the closest one was in Koper.

It is tough to let go of our habits, wherever we might go.

We longed to have a sugar-free drink in China, while my little family craved for dehydrated noodles with shrimp and were seemingly not tempted to try the fresh ones.

MAGI AND LARS

This lovely middle-aged couple and I immediately felt a friendly connection between us.

Before their arrival, I stopped in a small Karst village near Štorje on my way from Ljubljana to the coast and bought some homemade teran wine, which we then tried out eagerly that same evening. It is true that the coast is home to the white *malvazija*, but I am a big fan of the red *teran*, which is full of sediment and medicinal minerals. This dense fermented grape juice can only be produced on the modest Karst soil.

My two guests, who flew from the USA, were, naturally, also blown away by the rich aroma. Magi is an acclaimed writer of youth literature. She had received a literary award in Trento and since they were in the area, they decided to visit Slovenia as well. Lars lectures at university which allows him to have more freedom and free time to follow his gorgeous blonde wife on her book tours. Magi's ancestors came from Norway, which is where the blonde, almost white hair comes from, along with her warmth and openness.

They are avid hikers and they had already explored our short coastline in the first few days, so I invited them to visit some of the small villages further inland.

We breeze across Tartini Square, past the monastery and towards Arze.

This is the famous Venetian House? We thought it was the brick building on the other side of the square.

Oh no, that one is neo-Gothic, I lament. Ever since the Venetian House was given a new, bland coat of paint, this sort of confusion happens on a daily basis.

First, we head over to Krkavče, my little mystic village built on a large slab of bedrock. Due to its many water sources, it used to be known for the best washerwomen around. Before we reach the village, we are greeted by a village pond or *kal* on the left and a giant Istrian ox called *boškarin* on the right. It is, of course, hard to miss the famous *Krkavče Stone* and its ancient depiction of a person wearing a sun crown who looks across the peaceful Dragonja Valley towards the slope on the opposite side, topped by the village of Brič, while his other self keeps a watchful eye on the road that leads to the village.

The mysterious *menhir* is not in its original location anymore, which was confirmed to me when I visited it at the summer solstice, and the one in Krkavče is only a replica, the original sitting in some dark corner in a museum in Koper.

Unfortunately, the older the heritage of our ancestors, the less attention it gets.

We were greeted at the church, as per usual, by the friendly priest and keeper of this unusual temple, its surroundings decorated with corroded rocks, branches and flowers, which gives it a pagan and ancient feel. But what really stands out is the controversial double tomb of a former priest and his female cook in the narrow corridor next to the outer edge of the apse. All of this is a testament to the incredible tolerance of the people of Istria who always were and still are welcoming to foreigners as well as foreign novelties, but, at the same time, have upheld the customs of the old days.

We also visited Padna whose soft terrain presents a great antipode to the stone-based Krkavče. We were lucky to find that the doors of the Church of St. Blaise were not locked and we were able to take a peek inside. This is another place with a lot of traces of the old religion and its worshippers, and we were amazed by the blackened painting hidden behind the altar, waiting for a restoration team to bring it back to its former glory.

Magi and Lars are captivated by the peacefulness and the lovely thymus aroma, and by the distinctiveness that emanates from the Šavrini Hills. They still have many unknown paths to explore here one day.

That was enough impressions for one day.

Every afternoon, regardless of the day's events, Magi picks up her pen and sits down to write. Inspired by this steely discipline, I promise myself that I too shall follow her example. Someday.

BEATRICE AND ALFIO

They are so beautiful; two dark-skinned southerners with dark curly hair, so temperamental and happy.

I quickly find common ground with Beatrice since I just came from Apulia a month ago, which is where her grandmother is from. Lovely old towns, fairytale stone houses, the crystal clear sea – I have to admit that if I were in their shoes, I would find it difficult to vacation anywhere else.

In the evening, I catch the smell of marijuana coming from the garden. Alfio diligently rolls one joint after another and leans in towards Beatrice, speaking in a low voice.

Beatrice closes her eyes. She does not want Alfio to notice that she is on the verge of tears. She does not like drama, but his impulsiveness and mood swings in the past few months have really tired her out.

She tries to remember the beginnings when everything was bursting with passion. The image of Alfio bringing her cappuccino and croissants to bed, that silly expression of a powerless boy who won her over and ignited a desire in her that made her want to take his face in her hands and protect it.

She tries to remember the uncontrollable waves of laughter, the candlelit dinners, the playful dancing in the empty streets of Rome and the mischief they got up to. The slow undressing in the warm embrace of their home, his soft, hot lips on her skin.

Alfio's contorted face suddenly brings her back into the now. What does he even want? It takes her a few seconds to realise. He is angry, yelling at her for not listening. *Who is she thinking of? Her new lover? Is it Paolo?*

Beatrice explodes with anger. *Again with these delusions! Stop smoking this shit and you'll get rid of them!*

Alfio seems to have been waiting for her cue. Now he really lets himself go and, fuelled by rage, shouts at the top of his voice, slamming his fist on the table. When he finally realises after a dozen minutes or so that Beatrice has retreated into her shell and is not answering him anymore, he is overwhelmed with shame.

He is actually aware of how irritable he becomes when he runs out of marijuana, but he still believes that slamming the door behind him might save a little bit of his honour.

Early the next morning, Beatrice is ready to leave. She is waiting in the garden under the vine with her pink and blue suitcase and her tightened lips betray that a decision has been made. Alfio comes out behind her and looks at the ground when he shakes my hand. I give Beatrice a big firm hug to give her strength, woman to woman, in support of her decision.

SWEDISH GIRLS ARE AWESOME

Sofia keeps sending me texts to tell me where she is and when she is supposed to arrive, as if she was afraid of being left alone overnight in some weird place or even being stuck on the road.

That is when I receive a text from my daughter telling me that she is bringing a friend over. I immediately go out and buy fish for us three, but it later turned out that her friend was not coming.

As my daughter and I are preparing the fish in the afternoon, Sofia suddenly shows up at the door.

Great, we were missing one mouth!

She tells us stories of her months of travelling.

After she had finished her studies, she decided to see what is out there in the world before finding a job and maybe a partner.

I have to say I envy her a little bit. When I was her age, I was hoping I could do the same thing, but my parents were pushing me to find a job, so I ended up getting one even before I graduated. Once I got the job, it was really hard just giving it up.

Fortunately, there are plenty of options nowadays if you want to work while you travel.

Sofia has been doing a lot of volunteer work these past few months, the kind where only food and lodging is provided.

She spent the last few weeks in Dalmatia digging ditches on a remote island to provide the locals with a water supply. What joy and what a party there was at the grand opening!

No words can describe it! Nor can they describe the joy in the eyes of the old granny she was living with!

Before that, she cared for orphaned children with mental and physical disabilities in Turkey.

Her eyes start tearing up thinking about the little ones.

It was inconceivably hard to say goodbye!

Slowly, bit by bit, a bond forms between you and the children up until the moment when one of them gently rests his head on your shoulder and another one shyly takes your hand. I don't know if I could do it again! These children have already been abandoned by their parents and now they're being abandoned over and over again by volunteers. Sadly, there is not enough money for full-time teachers, for a more stable environment that the children so desperately need.

We both sink into silence, each in our own thoughts, watching the sky coming alive with the first stars of the evening.

In a perfect world, in a moment when everything stands still in silent gratitude and the sky merges with the sea into one unified blue, in this holy moment of timelessness, all discussions on fairness, chaos, sadness, disease, loneliness and abandonment somehow seem inappropriate, incompatible with the boundless beauty.

Sofia spends the last few days sunbathing by the sea or lounging on an inflatable beach mattress with her eyes closed, letting herself be lulled by the waves that will wash away all the traces of a journey she will never forget.

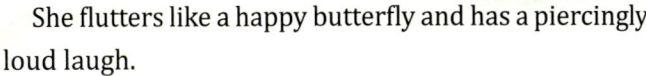

SVETLANA

She flutters like a happy butterfly and has a piercingly loud laugh.

She came alone, so I secretly keep an eye on her to see if she is bored, but it seems that is impossible with her.

She is always on the move; she goes for a swim along the coast every morning and evening, always at least an hour long.

A couple of days later, we go to Koper together since we both have errands to run there. During the drive, she tells me that a friend is coming over from Trieste to visit her and asks if it is okay if he stayed with her for two days.

Svetlana, a Russian, is a real vagabond. She drifts around the world and has lived in many places. She is a linguist and an etymologist, she studies old scripts, researches them and occasionally gives lectures. A child of the modern world if there ever was one, she could survive anywhere with her smarts.

She comes home with Dimitri late in the evening. I can hear them laughing and talking under the light of the moon.

Svetlana keeps pouring wine into the stemmed glasses that occasionally glow with a blood red colour in the candlelight.

Dimitri is excitedly explaining something and flailing with his arms while she sips from her glass and keeps moving closer and closer. *Aha, mmm, mmm ...* She brushes against his hand with her cleavage ever so lightly, but he pretends not to notice.

The next morning, Svetlana gets up unusually early. She fries eggs, slices tomatoes and cucumbers for the salad, and prepares the cheese and bread. She sings passionately and gracefully dances around the kitchen. While coffee is bubbling in the moka pot, she sets the table.

Still yawning, Dimitri joins her at the table. It only takes a few sips of coffee to reignite the debate from last night. This time, she contributes to the discussion a bit, also adding her distinct piercing laugh and her sensual interjections, *aha, mmm, aha.*

One more evening is ahead of them, their last here in Piran. Is it just me or are her cooing sounds becoming more and more sensual and erotic? They are inviting, suggestive and seductive.

Once again, Dimitri is the one doing all the talking all evening and late into the night with his deep, snappy voice.

All of her efforts are completely focused on one thing and one thing only.

Svetlana

In my mind, I wish her a sultry night.

Svetlana listens to him absent-mindedly, just enough to be able to confirm something by nodding or adding a gentle remark at the right time. She thinks of the years of studying and all the hard work put into her doctorate, the endless series of sleepless nights spent at the keyboard with a cup of coffee in hand. So much effort, proving herself, preparations.

She made it and she is grateful for it.

But still… she wants a husband, children, she wants a real home.

She observes Dimitri's Greek profile with an accentuated nose and ruffled black beard, palms with thin white fingers which emphasise every word spoken with their restless motion, underlining it on an invisible piece of paper.

Would he be the right one for me?

She slides even closer to him and, in a seemingly meaningless motion, presses her leg against his.

It seems that, once again, he does not notice it, but after a while he readjusts himself – feigning indifference – to the right, very slightly, just enough to avoid touching her.

In the morning, we accidentally miss each other as they are in a hurry to catch the boat to Trieste. I enter the apartment and glance over to the beds which stand miles apart from each other.

Since I have been hosting people, no one has ever put them so far apart.

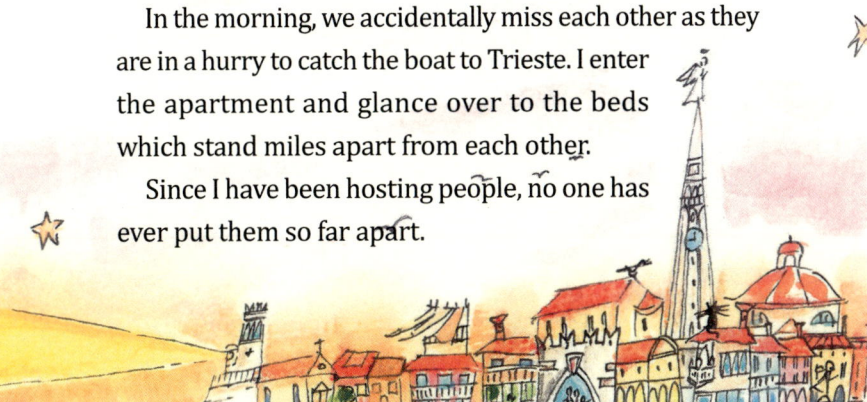

As summer turns into autumn, I get fewer and fewer guests. It is finally time for that long awaited season ... The roles are reversed and I can finally dust off my suitcase and start planning my own holiday.
I look for budget flights and interesting accommodation, mostly with the help of Airbnb.
Not so long ago, I would have simply bought a plane ticket and went with the flow, but now I enjoy trying out these new possibilities and meeting new hosts.

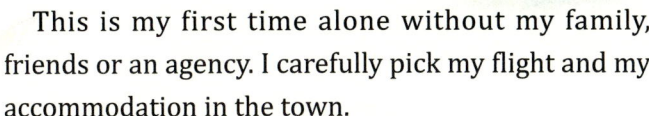

ANTALYA, TURKEY

This is my first time alone without my family, friends or an agency. I carefully pick my flight and my accommodation in the town.

This story actually does not belong here since this was before Booking.com and Airbnb.

It was a time when you first checked the Lonely Planet guidebook under the heading *accommodation* – in my case, it was under the subheading *budget* – and hoped that the featured family pensions also had a website that would allow you to book a room. I managed to find such a family hotel two weeks before my flight and I sent them an inquiry via e-mail. I then impatiently waited for a reply and kept checking my e-mail every day, but it did not come.

Already pretty worried, I sent another inquiry:

Is my reservation confirmed?

The next day, all I received was a sparse reply:

Reservation o. k.

I remember how uneasy I felt when we finally touched down in Antalya a few days later. It was a chartered flight from Ljubljana and upon landing, all the other passengers lined up and headed towards a bus that was already waiting to take them to their hotel. For a moment, the thought of joining the back end of this procession crossed my mind, but I quickly snapped out of it and headed off, all by myself, through a door to the other side of the airport, the exiled ugly duckling.

Out front, I waved to a taxi and, after a few minutes, the anxiety was gone.

I was dropped off in front of my accommodation in a narrow little street in the old town and the driver waited with me for someone to come open the door. I was greeted by a friendly-looking grey-haired old man with a big smile and a twinkle in his eye.

Merhaba! Ben ingilizce konuşmıyorum! No English!

We gave each other a big smile. I now knew why there was no initial response to my e-mail and why the one I eventually received was so short. Their son usually takes care of this, but he is currently not here.

The days went by and I had a great time, riding around in *dolmuş* vans, visiting Cappadocia, the Anatolian Plateau, and the Lycian tombs on the coast. I have met some locals and was very happy and grateful that I was there alone going through a bunch of new experiences.

It is sometimes difficult to let go of the reservations of a frightened child and allow yourself to venture out of your comfort zone into adventures that remind us that we are alive.

The grey old man and an old woman would sit at the table in the courtyard early each morning and prepare a delicious breakfast for everyone living in their home.

Their son, who is a nice young man, came home on the last day of my holiday. He told me of his journey in excellent English and had a good laugh at my expense for having doubts over the e-mail correspondence.

In the morning, the kind old man took me to the airport. We were friends by this point, so he gave me a sincere hug as a goodbye.

The Siwa Oasis, Egypt

I have never experienced any serious difficulties while travelling. I was never robbed or had my wallet stolen; to be honest, everyone has always been incredibly nice and no one has done anything remotely bad to me.

Not only that, but on my way to Cappadocia, I even left my backpack with my wallet and documents at a roadside inn where we had stopped. When I noticed this after a good ten minutes, we went back and my backpack – all alone, leaning against the backrest of a chair on a giant terrace which, not long ago, was packed with people – was waiting for me, untouched.

In a similar act of forgetfulness, my daughter and I once left a brand new video camera at a roadside inn in China. It was also waiting for us in the same place when we came back to get it.

Otherwise, I usually never leave documents and money in my room, I always take them with me.

My first journey to another continent, visiting Egypt, was unusual in many ways.

We finished our trip with a stop at the Siwa Oasis, the famous oasis that hosted Alexander the Great when he visited the famous oracle in the Temple of Amun.

It was a long drive from Alexandria and we reached our accommodation – a group of small shacks in a camp –

when it was already pitch dark. After a very delicious dinner, followed by a shisha smoking session, we felt our way to our beds and fell asleep.

Very early in the dark of the morning, before sunrise, I was awoken by a special symphony – the roosters were joined in their wake-up call by nearby donkeys, some also chiming in from the more remote parts of the village. *How moving and sad is the harmonious cacophony of these poor slaves. What are they so passionately conversing about?* I thought to myself. *Forever beaten, laden with great weight on their backs. Maybe they too are waiting to be freed from Egyptian slavery?*

I was completely awakened by the peculiar beauty of this early morning reveille. I got up to take a look at our dessert home in the still of the coming morning. I went for a walk along the paths between the huts and ran into a young Egyptian man along the way. I greeted him casually and made my way into the bathrooms. When I locked myself inside the first stall, I noticed a shadow cast by a pair of legs. Someone was silently strolling outside of the stalls, so I waited until I was alone before I returned to my hut. I collapsed onto the bed and immediately fell asleep. Soon, I was awakened by the faint rattling of the lock. The padlock of our hut would not close properly as it had not been oiled in a while. I then heard the muffled squeaking of the door as it slowly began to open.

All my friends know that being loud is not my thing, but this time I made an exception and yelled at the poor boy so fiercely (the one I had just ran into on the path) that I did not only frighten him, but myself as well. After he ran away, I blocked the door with everything I could find and slowly fell asleep again.

At breakfast, I smiled at the guide who last night so confidently claimed that the ladies can finally relax as the oasis is well known for its local gay population. *Next time you bring people here, save that comment for yourself, although – as the saying goes – there are exceptions to every rule!*

Later in the sunny morning, when events become clearer, I realised that I had probably made eye contact at our first meeting – considered very indecent in these parts (let us put aside the fact that I am also as blind as a bat without my contact lenses).

In the afternoon, the owner of the camp offered us a donkey ride free of charge (I am not sure if the guide told him about my morning encounter). These were the smallest and mangiest donkeys I have ever seen. Some of them were more than willing to cooperate, others did it after having a long think about it and receiving a hefty bribe, while some chose ignorant sabotage that probably would have ended with punishment on some other occasion, but this time resulted only in laughter, some petting and the luckiest of them all were even given an apple or two!

BALI, INDONESIA

Emboldened by my first attempt, I decide to go on another solo vacation next summer, this time to Bali. I have heard so many things about this paradise that I want to see it with my own eyes (the intoxicating Gudang Garam clove cigarettes also helped to tip the scales).

After some weird flight complications, changed flight paths, delays and twisting loops, I finally make it to Seminyak, Bali's cosmopolitan resort, where a modest little room in a family guesthouse is waiting for me.

I am greeted by a tall, beautiful woman with a classically refined face and I simply cannot hide my astonishment over the perfection of her appearance. She tells me she is from Java.

The sun is already setting above the coast of infinite sand dunes. As far as the eye can see, there is just one long beach, the colourful kite sails, the laughter of children running to and fro. I would love to go for a swim, but it seems that the sea is too shallow even after walking for miles, so I only go for a quick dip in this shallow muddy stew. I take a quick look around the town centre and return to my room. I can hear loud German toasting coming from the terrace below, but nothing, not even a giant tropical cockroach in my luggage, can prevent me from having my well-deserved sleep.

In the morning, the enticing aroma of the small Balinese pancakes fills the house.

The beautiful woman is here again. I have a chat with a young German traveller sitting at the table next to mine. I am told this guesthouse is owned by an older German man who was celebrating yesterday, right here on this terrace. The girl is also his.

Aha, she is also his property, I cannot help but to be cynical.

When I was picking my accommodation, I was drawn in by the description that used words like *homely, local, Balinese.* Now, the fact that people are still being *bought –* more subtly, but still – gives me an uneasy feeling, so I decide to leave and head north that same day.

In the hopes of contributing to the well-being of a local even just a little, I give a nod to the first driver that offers me transportation. He is a handsome young man, but he only speaks a few words of English.

Me very good. I come you room tonight.

Whoa! Do you know I'm old enough to be your mother?

Really? How old?

When I tell him, he does not say anything for quite a while and ponders over the received information. His mother is younger.

Then, as if suddenly struck with amnesia, he starts again:

I come you room tonight.

Just drive, no talking! I respond curtly.

In Singaraja, he recommends a place to stay. They are his *good friends*, naturally. Here, the roles are reversed.

An older English woman runs the guesthouse together with her younger Balinese husband.

Everyone seems to be resigned to – or even pleased with – this new form of *colonialism* and it is obviously not meant for me to save their world. After all, similar relationships exist where I come from, they are just more noticeable here because they are so common.

I indulge in the wonderful beaches, swimming in warm pools under waterfalls, the greenness of the rice fields, the sound of *gamelan* in the evenings, the mysterious stories of the shadow puppets, the intoxicating aroma of durians, all the lightness of floating in paradise. A paradise with only one fault – it seems to have somehow bypassed the locals.

MARRAKECH, MOROCCO

Some time ago, I did a group tour of Morocco. I promised myself then that I would return to Marrakech one day, specifically to the picturesque and impressively large Jemaa el-Fna Square. There, you can get anything your heart desires and see wonders worthy of the Arabian One Thousand and One Nights. Snake charmers (they actually keep them on ice all the time so that they go numb and are not dangerous), monkey charmers, musical groups from Mali or from other parts of North Africa, storytellers (they always have plenty of listeners), fortune tellers, juice and tea sellers, Bedouin women with tattooed faces who paint your hands with henna ...

I have seen many Asian *souks*, but I can say with confidence that none are as colourful as this one.

Riad Ada in Medina is tucked away at the end of a dark street and the first impression left me a little worried as to how I was going to feel coming home in the blackness of the night.

Like at home, Hasni shrugs. *Right*, I think to myself, *my street in Piran is also quiet and dark, maybe my guests also find it quite scary when they first arrive.*

When I adopt this different perspective, the fear is gone. The street becomes homely and my daughter and I breathe a sigh of relief every time we get near our Marrakech *home*.

The city is full of such *riads*, small family hotels. The buildings are designed according to an ancient model, always featuring a small courtyard in the middle where the whole family sits while working or socialising. The upper floors have two or three rooms each and the roof is where you have a mandatory terrace with a beautiful view of the city. This is where they nap in the hot hours of the afternoon or rest in the evenings, drinking tea, smoking shisha...

It is most magical at sunset when the call to prayer *Allahu Akbar* sounds from all the minarets. To improve on the first impression, Hasni offers us a room on the terrace, incomparable to the others – airy and full of sounds and smells that you can only experience here. We are awakened by the chirping of finches who have perfected an incredibly dangerous technique of free falling into the courtyard where they pick up crumbs and other leftovers before they shoot up into the sky, shrieking loudly.

All houses have similar terraces, full of life and activity. I recall the many stories of the Maghreb writers describing how infatuated youths would stand on such terraces, trying desperately to catch a glimpse of their girlfriends because they could not see their uncovered faces elsewhere.

In the evening, Hasni, a handsome young man in his thirties, invites us to have a drink before bed.

He tells us that he runs two *riads* that are owned by his extended family. He sometimes sleeps in this one, sometimes in the other one. He makes sure that the employed housewives prepare breakfast for guests, he goes to the bazaar to get food, and he takes care of the website and communicates with guests. With a soft, melodic voice with no accent, he describes a life that seems a bit monotonous for a young man his age. I might be imagining it, but I sense this undefined longing, an unfulfilled desire emanating from his words.

The next few evenings bring more guests and he invites each of them to share an evening drink with him where he whispers with his soft, calm voice the predictable story of his life.

SIENA, ITALY

During the New Year's holidays, I was suddenly overcome by a desire to visit Siena. I got into my car in the early morning hours and by lunchtime, I was already in Tuscany.

I have only been to Siena once before and it was a really quick stop.

I still remember how awestruck I was on my first visit when I stepped from a narrow little street onto the unexpectedly vast Piazza del Campo.

I immediately recognised it as the magical square I have visited so many times in my childhood dreams. I remembered how I used to sit with the other children on the steps in front of a house – at the time, I perceived it as my own – just opposite the beautiful town palace, which was very far away from my perspective. The warm brick ground and the yellowy ochre buildings, the colourful clothing, the old toys. We would sometimes play and run around in the nearby streets and other times we would sit in silence and watch the maidens and knights with their exquisite silk and brocade clothing, rustling as they glided past us. That was when I would feel a rush of anxiety mixed with a child's faith in a perfect future – imagine how fun it will be when I grow up to be a maiden like that! Then, I too will grab my lord under his arm and proudly parade along the edge of the piazza!

After all these decades, I can still bring up some of the dream sequences; that is how deeply they are imprinted into me – more real than reality itself.

As I stood there in that *déjà vu* moment, surprised that the place from my dreams really existed, I wanted to bring up as much detail as possible.

I ordered a cappuccino in a nearby café and immersed myself into the sensate impressions of the place, became one with it. After a few moments, I felt like I could locate the house in front of which I had sat so many times in my dreams. I stood up to touch the door handle on the faded door to relive its touch. It was then that the door opened unexpectedly and a small old lady with a walking stick stepped out onto the square. The door creaked as it slowly closed behind her and it gave me just enough time to catch a quick glimpse of the grand staircase and the colours of the floor tiles assembled into a diamond pattern. The inside of the house did not speak to me, however, with the possible exception of the brick colour of the tiles, which I remember from my dreams and have always really liked.

Ever since then, I wanted to visit the town again, maybe unearth another buried memory. After a few years, I was here again. Unfortunately, I realised that I could not relive much more than some unspecified moments linked to a small square, the *contrades* and the *Palio*. What would it have been like if I had the chance to see this as a child, could I have expanded my *memories* to more scenes?

I stayed in Siena for a week and I spent my last night before departure in the little town of Colle di Val d'Elsa.

In the morning, I first visited Volterra – a walled town, once an important seat of the Etruscans, but now known as *The City of Vampires* thanks to the popular Twilight Saga. The town has this strange gloom about it which definitely helps with its reputation.

After several hours of walking around, I called it a day and drove past San Gimignano towards my temporary home, finally arriving there just as darkness was setting. The ancient palace seemed silent and abandoned, and despite banging the knockers, nobody showed up. I called the host on my mobile phone and shortly after, a handsome dark-haired young man appeared. The giant palace actually was as abandoned as it seemed. We walked past an enormous and empty dining room and then climbed the steps to my little room. It was almost higher than it was wide and I have never seen windows so tall before. I put down my luggage and went back into the street with my host.

What a grand palace! I exclaimed, not hiding my surprise. *Does anyone live here?*

Oh, no, he smiled, *it's owned by the nuns from the monastery down the road*, he waved his hand randomly, *they just rent out rooms to tourists.*

And what do you do, I was curious.

I came from Romania and the sisters offered me a job as a receptionist …

As I was lying in bed a few hours later, everything seemed so bizarre to me and I just could not decide if it was funny or scary. I could hear the wood creaking now and then, and I could occasionally hear the front door being opened and then closed with a loud bang every time, after which everything was quiet once again. I noticed there was a small door in the wall close to the ceiling, probably some kind of storage, but it was too high to take a peek and see what was behind it. It could have been anything, or even anyone.

I also did not dare to try and open the four-metre-high windows – they were too heavy if something went wrong. And my host from Romania … is he maybe in some way connected to Count Dracula?

I finally got around to seeing the town in the morning, a perfectly preserved medieval nest. Instant tourism has not yet spoiled it like San Gimignano on the neighbouring hill. A little disappointed that I did not meet a single vampire, I said goodbye to the young man from Romania. Looking at his smile in the morning light, it was clear that his perfect teeth did not include any pointy canines …

Apulia, Italy /
Gianna and Antonio

It was at the beginning of my journey as an Airbnb host, before the season even started, that I travelled to the heel of the Italian boot with my three girlfriends. I could not help myself, naturally, so I used the Airbnb platform to find a few places to stay before we left. I was interested in seeing how other people do it, what they offer and how much time they spend with their guests.

The first thing that comes to mind when you think of Apulia, for most people at least, is their *trulli*, the distinct round stone huts; such houses are called *kažun* in Istria, the only difference being that the Apulian ones are larger as they were meant to be lived in on a daily basis and were not just used as temporary shelter for shepherds. In the past, big families used to live there since these non-taxed *never finished homes* were the only ones they could afford due to poverty. In those days, every village used to have watchmen who would alert people as soon as they saw a tax collectors approaching from afar so that the villagers could take shingles off roofs to avoid paying taxes.

Our first hosts, Gianna and Antonio, own such a *trullo*, to which they added several additional rooms, while the central stone section with a high dome and a fireplace set against the wall remains a place for socialising. The most beautiful part of their large and remote property is the wonderful garden with fruit trees, hammocks and comfortable lawn chairs scattered all around.

Since we arrived on a Sunday and could not pick up our rental car, it took quite a few lifts for Antonio to first take us to our new home, then back to the nearby Martina Franca for a short tour and then back home again.

We find it amusing how hard they are trying to fulfil their roles to the highest standards. They are both teachers and this is part of their characters – they are very sweet, but always striving for complete control and the desire for perfection.

The next morning, we rent a small red fiat. Our little *trullo* becomes a cosy home and our base for visiting the nearby and distant points of interest. First, we visited Alberobella, of course, the capital of the *trulli*, and then the ancient Matera. Due to our base's remoteness, the navigation Antonio lent us would have been an essential tool, especially in the first couple olk other time when we badly needed it, which is why we sometimes spent a long time wandering around the countryside, trying to find our refuge.

Gianna also prepared bikes for us. I sometimes go for a ride down the abandoned street early in the morning, not once seeing a single person. Only one original farmhouse still remains, all others are now holiday homes that only come alive in the summer.

On our last evening, our hosts invite themselves over. There is a barbecue out back and they drop us a hint that they expect us to prepare something on our last day and share our impressions with them. However, we get so distracted in the late afternoon, admiring the mesmerising town of Monopoli with its majestic walls bathing in the magical light of the setting sun that we have to postpone our return to base. After an hour, we are finally on our way home where Gianna and Antonio are already waiting for us at the door with a packet of traditional Apulian sweets. They seem a bit perplexed as they look over to the empty table, apparently used to a different kind of catering. With a joint effort, we manage to rustle up some quick snacks and get comfortable in the lawn chairs, while they get ready for some *small talk* with a burst of questions which seem to have been prepared in advance. We dutifully go over the usual topics like work, family, travel, our impressions of Apulia, and the adventures of the last few days.

We are in good spirits and we toast frequently. Antonio is cracking jokes when turning to my friend Nadja – am I imagining things or do I sense a bit of tension with

Gianna? I think I notice her readjusting herself uncomfortably in her chair as she shoots the next question:

Where did you meet? Have you been friends a long time?

Well, Sanja chuckles, *Nadja and I met in a very unusual way. After years of being married, my husband found a new woman and left. It was a difficult time, but, at the same time, it was not that surprising as I could sense that he was occasionally seeing other women.*

A few years after the divorce, he fell in love again – with Nadja.

The children met her first when they were visiting their father and, eventually, we met as well. However, the story repeated itself. My ex-husband, the incorrigible butterfly that he is, he flew away from Nadja as well.

We eventually became good friends and when we look back now, we often laugh at the memories of our shared man, the sultan! He really knew how to be charming in order to put a spell on both of us. Nadja is a fantastic person! I really love her!

Gianna almost chokes on a piece of marzipan cake. They both fall silent for a few moments and we observe them playfully.

Would anyone like some tea? Nadja asks.

Thank you, but, you know, I have work tomorrow, Antonio tries to excuse himself.

They do not hide their astonishment very well as they head back to their car. We drink Nadja's tea and continue talking into the night.

Is it better to tell the truth or to lie? Would you have chosen hate instead of love if you were in Sanja's shoes?

Ah, the primitivo wine under the Apulian sky ...

SUZANA

Suzana and I only talked over the phone when we were in Lecce trying to find, unsuccessfully, the address she gave us. Our troubles stemmed from the fact that two streets in that town had the same name and it is, of course, easier to find the wrong one. We sat down, in desperation, under the shade of a tree in front of the wrong home to wait for her father to come and get us. When he later led us to the right place, we unanimously concluded that we never could have found the street by ourselves.

It was worth the effort, though. The wonderful apartment right next to the historical centre of a majestic city that people like to call the Florence of the South completely captivated us. The most inspiring were the colourful expressionist paintings hung in all the rooms. This is why Suzana liked to call her apartment *the gallery*.

We were greeted in the kitchen by her mother. We quickly found out that her parents are divorced, but they are grudgingly trying to make it work for the sake of their daughter. The father's liveliness subsided a little when next to his ex-wife, but he still waited patiently to see if she was going to show us everything we needed to know. The apartment is full of locks, each requiring a special technique to get it to open, then there is the anxious neighbours, Wi-Fi passwords, fussy modems ... the tricks of modern-day living, you could say.

They tackled all of this with a lot of courage, readjusting their glasses as they were trying to catch a beam of light across the modem to help them make out the tiny letters of the additional password, trying to remember how the remote works or where the fuse box is.

They were connected in this wonderfully modern, high-tech apartment by the lovely shared concern for their daughter. Meeting her, however, was seemingly slipping away.

Ah, sorry, something came up (my fiancé invited me out to dinner), I won't be coming over tonight.

Oh, you'd like to stay an extra day? Great, my mom will come and collect the payment, I'm still busy, unfortunately.

As all mothers, I have been there before. However, I can also remember very well how fiercely I resisted all these parental favours in my thirties. I thought that I was being suffocated and that they were not allowing me to grow up.

Elena and Cosimo

They actually do not belong among the true Airbnb stories since we only found their apartment on arrival after being dissatisfied with the one we had booked online. It was a few kilometres from the city centre, located in a concrete suburb built for summer tourism, but when we entered Gallipoli and got a taste of its atmosphere, we did not want to leave. If I may draw a comparison – the difference was much like the one between Portorož and Piran.

We spent most of the day walking around and getting lost in the narrow streets, admiring the dark cellars – oil mills, embedded deep into the earth, and even went for a swim in the afternoon heat at a lovely beach in the small town bay.

It was getting late, though, and that finally forced us to start looking for a new place to stay.

We split up into two small groups, but Nadja got lucky and immediately ran into Cosimo.

A small, friendly man with a thin eagle-like nose and a shy smile, he looked as frail as one of the precious vases in his mansion, a stark contrast to his better and much heavier half, *signora* Elena, a lively, loud and determined matron.

We managed to get the last two vacant rooms and since there was four of us, they split us into two pairs and put us into two separate palaces.

And what palaces they were! The first one was the older of the two, located right on the main street next to the cathedral, boasting a worn stone staircase and lavish rooms in sunny yellow tones decorated with stucco and old frescoes, and was the original family home with all the valuables and memories accumulated over the centuries of glorious history. The second one, a more classicist building, but no less luxurious, full of works of art, precious carved wooden furniture, Venetian mirrors and secret passageways, was located a few blocks towards the south.

As Cosimo was putting us into the guestbook, Elena came rushing in to task him with some other work, but he coldly dodged this new assignment, *Can't you see I'm busy?*

Exhausted, Elena collapsed onto her ducal throne, which creaked under her weight, and got to work herself, still breathing heavily.

Where would you like to have breakfast? In the first or the second palace?

We chose the first. The next morning, we noticed that they each reign in their own nest. Cosimo is the heir of an old noble family, basically everything belongs to him. Despite this, he gave the first palace to Elena and he takes care of the second (to be honest, he spent most of his time during our stay watching football in peace, which could not have been achieved so easily in the first palace). *How cunning*, we mused. Due to her great weight, Elena probably does not even go out and it is hard to imagine her walking over to the second palace – this is where Cosimo can have his peace.

It is, however, a great partnership, I think to myself. *Cosimo is like some creature from a forgotten time, gentle and educated, while Elena is incredibly industrious! Without her skills, the two palaces probably would have fallen into ruin, but they are successfully maintaining them and they even received international funds for the restoration of cultural heritage.*

Instead of bread, we were served old toast for breakfast (*probably dating back to the construction of the manor?* Nadja guessed). Elena showed us how to soften it in lukewarm water and pour olive oil over it, which is an old Apulian dish, very handy for long boat journeys and discovering distant lands.

On our final morning, we asked Elena if we could print out our boarding passes. She took me to her quarters – a small room with a bathroom and a large bed, where she can rest discreetly, especially when Cosimo is elsewhere …

She then gave us a tour of the really tastefully decorated former main salon which is off limits for guests, probably due to its value, and drew our attention to the centuries-old crib, where Cosimo spent his first nights in this world.

Was I just imagining it or did her voice tremble with subdued tenderness?

Palestine and Israel, Jerusalem

Back in Jerusalem, the city of golden domes, secrets, the endless river of tears and intolerance and dedicated piety. I really want to see it again and show it to my daughter.

The magic of the ancient city has sparked inside of me, just like in countless other hearts, a love for white palaces, underground labyrinths, lively *souks* and places that we, raised in Christian tradition as well as people belonging to the two other Abrahamic religions – Judaism and Islam, hear stories of in our youth.

Even though I do not belong to any religion in particular, rather to all of them or a little bit to each, I get a lump in my throat every time I walk up Via Dolorosa to Golgotha or when I touch the Star of Bethlehem in the Church of the Nativity or the stone monolith at Christ's tomb, where the hands of so many pilgrims have touched the marble that they have left marks in it.

The shocking beauty reveals itself in the redness of the setting sun which colours the white marble of the Jewish patriarchs' tombs and the marble Tomb of Absalom, the lost son of David and brother of Solomon, at the foot of the Mount of Olives.

For he said, I have no son to keep my name in remembrance: and he called the pillar after his own name: and it is called unto this day, Absalom's place.

Probably the most striking is the golden dome of Al Aqsa, a shrine on the Temple Mount which you can only visit during limited hours in the morning because of arbitrary political decisions. The intricately designed calligraphy of the prayers etched on blue tiles: *La ilaha illallah Muhammadur rasulullah ...* Is it even possible that some Zionists want to demolish this otherworldly beauty and build in its place the Third Temple?

We spent few nights in Jerusalem in a hostel which turned out to be not the best idea, but most of the affordable apartments were already booked because of the Christmas holidays. On our last night, we finally had enough of our mouldy storage room on the terrace (they advertised it as a 2-bedroom with a bathroom ... what a joke!) and found another hostel near the Damascus Gate in the Muslim Quarter which I stayed in before. We were lucky and were able to book the last remaining room. Since my last visit, its industrious owners have transformed it into a lovely hotel with probably one of the best views from the rooftop terrace. The panoramic view encompasses the entire city: the silver and gold domes of the basilicas and mosques, the Mount of Olives, the rolling mists in the background. The dozens and dozens of rooftop terraces are crammed so tightly together that they look like a human anthill, each with its different inhabitants: women hanging out clothes to dry, children playing or crying, families sitting around in the cool of the evening, people showing guests views of the city. I could spend years on this terrace, but our time was up.

In the second leg of our journey, we set off for the Sea of Galilee where we finally found some small rooms to our liking.

KALED

We had booked our first Airbnb accommodation in Nazareth.

Remembering this story still makes me blush to this day ... Let me say in my defence that the first impression of the city was all but pleasant. Leaving Jerusalem alone was enough to dampen my spirits. After many hours of travelling, the bus driver dropped us off at a roundabout next to a shopping centre. We were quite disappointed when we realised that the mighty Basilica of the Annunciation was still quite far away. We trudged our heavy luggage uphill past many shoddy car repair workshops and kept asking along the way for the address we were given. Many buildings on the street were abandoned with shattered windows – as if a bomb attack happened the day before – and I kept hoping that we would not end up in one of these dumps. Out of breath, we finally made it to another roundabout with a modern well under the top of the hill, which is where our apartment should be. *It's going to be tough,* a friendly waiter said after we had ordered some tea, *the street doesn't have house numbers. Anyway, this is the street,* he pointed in the direction we had just come from. *Oh, no*, I groaned. We called Kaled again and he came to pick us up after ten minutes. Still under the impression of the dirty street, I plodded behind him sceptically. We navigated an abandoned labyrinth of unfinished garages until we finally reached an outside staircase and walked up to the spacious apartment. This is where we had our room and the shared bathroom and kitchen.

Hmm, how do I lock the room? I inquired, once I had closed the sliding door. *You don't,* he shrugged.

I felt chills run down my spine, mostly because I was mad at myself for carelessly dragging my daughter into this adventure. It did not help put my mind at ease that Kaled had a cultured chat with us and gave us tips on what to see and where to go for food. It did not help that he made us a proper Italian espresso and even showed us his notary office.

All this time, all I could do was think about that sorry door. *How are we going to lock it? What if he brings friends into the apartment? After all, we can't know for sure that what he told us about himself is actually true ...* I rummaged frantically through the bazaar, which was already closing, trying to find something useful that could be used to fasten the door handles. With a lot of effort, I managed to find a linen trouser belt, shoelaces and some other similar items.

We then ran into another problem. We have had no issues withdrawing money from our credit cards in Jerusalem, but it simply would not work here. We spent the entire afternoon looking for the right bank or cash machine and only managed to find one once darkness had already fallen. We then finally toured the city a bit, which suddenly revealed itself in all its magical atmosphere.

We kept putting off returning to our apartment quite late into the evening, but the moment finally came. Not in the least pleased with the whole situation, we slipped past the scary underground garages to the staircase.

We unlocked the empty apartment and I immediately started meticulously scrutinising the sliding doors. *Ah, there is no key, but they can actually be locked with a bolt!* Relieved and tired, we collapsed onto our beds and immediately fell asleep. We did not even notice when Kaled came home.

The next morning, re-energised and full of optimism, we could only smile at our fears from the day before.

What goes on in our heads... fear really is a powerful thing ...

JON

Early in the afternoon, we made our way from Nazareth to Tiberias, a town on the shores of the Sea of Galilee, which is known as the main coastal tourist town. After the painful experience of dragging our luggage from the day before, I stubbornly insisted that we take a taxi, which turned out to be a good decision since we later discovered that Jon's home lies on top of a hill. His terrace offers an incredible view of the still surface of the lake, which was already covered with an early afternoon mist.

All of Israel seemed to us somehow old-fashioned, disorderly. As if people stopped caring for buildings once they were built. You can see plaster coming off houses, unkempt surroundings, the grass is out of control, the gardens full of junk. Jon's house has also seen better days, although you can feel at every step that he tries his best with his limited resources to do the essential maintenance.

The room is spacious with a private bathroom. The furniture is exactly what I remember from the sixties or seventies, but it is sparkling clean. We are really surprised at how attentive our host is regarding his business, making sure everything is washed, the linens smell nice, the bathroom is spotless, everything attests to his attention to detail. It is completely different compared to the other places we have stayed in so far.

In the evening, we make tea and sit on the terrace with a beautiful view of the lake and the Golan Heights in the distance. Jon explains that room letting is an important source of income for him and that he earns additional money doing odd jobs. A nice, long-haired young man, he studied psychology, but decided not to pursue it anymore. He now enjoys living at home, going for walks ... Behind his house is a winding trail very popular with hikers called the *Jesus Trail*. The next morning, we decide to give the trail a try and follow it to Mount Berenice where we realise that we have become quite taken with the semi-desert landscape and immediately regret having to leave so soon as we would have loved to explore it for at least one more day. The mountains are covered with sparse vegetation and the ochre red soil is intersected with trails. Here and there, you hear the jingling of the bells hanging from the neck of a ram and its herd. It is like being transported into biblical times and I can easily imagine a long-haired youth from two thousand years ago, travelling in the calm of the dreamy landscape and effortlessly covering the short distances between the settlements on the coast of the Sea of Galilee, which reflects in the sun like a mirage. This local youth could easily have taken on Jon's appearance, a young man with dreadlocks and fiery black eyes. He would explore the dusty paths as he does today, happy in the embrace of the landscape that he knows and belongs to.

While drinking tea, we touch upon the coexistence of the Jews and the Palestinians. Jon answers calmly and I sense none of that intolerance that I detected just five years ago talking to young Israelis. Much like with Kaled, a Palestinian from Nazareth, this question has hardly touched him. He simply wants to live his life, just like young people all around the world. Jon's view is a tad more philosophical, unique and fanciful than Kaled's, but there is no place for hatred in it. There are, of course, still some leftovers of the half-truths embedded into young people by the education system and politics, but it seems that the militant aggression of the previous generations has no place in today's world anymore. Fingers crossed!

EDI AND ADI

We spend New Year's Eve in Tel Aviv where we finish our tour of Palestine and Israel. We have been texting back and forth with Edi since morning because he is at work and we do not want to bother him by calling. He will leave the key in the mailbox. Even with the help of the taxi driver, we have great trouble finding the address and we are successful only after we are given extensive and precise directions by our host.

The apartment is very nice, minimalistic, a few vintage pieces really add to the charm of it. I admire the orderliness of the home, the cooking utensils, the bathroom supplies, the furniture, the fixtures ... How is it possible that men are so good at this?

Edi and Adi are a loving gay couple. There is a notice next to the front door saying they will be celebrating their wedding in five days!

We are pleasantly surprised by a note with a friendly *welcome* and our names on it, plus two pieces of chocolate. A charming touch!

We head to the coast and make for Jaffa. Walking barefoot and wading through the small waves and the softness of the sand, we manage to reach it in about an hour or two. We walk across the entire bay – our home is at its northernmost point and our destination all the way in the south.

To celebrate the departure of the old year, we each order a St. Peter's Fish (tilapia), which we had already seen on menus in many restaurants along the Sea of Galilee. Unfortunately, we thought that the pictures of the large fish on the menu were just a marketing trick and since we were already quite full after the hummus and other snacks, we just barely manage to finish them. We later notice that other guests order one fish for two people.

The little narrow streets of Jaffa are magical, I could spend hours getting lost in them. This port town is one of the oldest in the world – according to a legend, it was established by Noe's son Japheth. It comes as no surprise, therefore, that it survived so many different governments, and all the arrivals and departures of peoples, which I find quite comforting. From this perspective, the recent exile of Arabic merchants from the old town is just a small detail from its rich history book, which has undoubtedly not been finished yet.

We finally meet our hosts in the evening. They are both very kind and talkative, and they seem so similar in their appearance as well as their mannerisms and lively gestures.

Tel Aviv is a multicultural city and it's very modern and tolerant. Here, we live side by side with each other with no problem whatsoever. Jerusalem is a completely different story – that's where all the religious zealots are, they explain. *That's why we can't even imagine living there.*

Edi and Adi are just two creative young men who want to live in this nice part of the world in peace, just like their peers elsewhere.

We have to get up before six in the morning. The friendly Edi gets up with us and calls us a taxi. As we are leaving, he stands on the doorstep in his underwear for quite some time, still half asleep and shivering, waving us goodbye.

What a nice young man, the taxi driver remarks.

I wave back – to Edi and Adi, Jon, Kaled, Jerusalem and Al Aqsa, Ein Gedi, Gaza, Jericho, to every single person in this beautiful country that has it all, peace being the only thing that seems to keep eluding it.

LAURA

After we had finished watching the film *Shun Li and the Poet*, starring the amazing Rade Šerbedžija, with my friends, we looked at each other, all thinking the same thing: *Let's go to Chioggia!*

We planned our route, added a visit to the Po River Delta, including a mandatory tasting of the local eels, and set the date of departure. Unfortunately, we could not make it work on our first try and on our second attempt – after even more unexpected complications – only me and Sanja actually travelled.

Our accommodation was in the new part of town in Sottomarina, on a different islet, actually.

Laura skilfully manoeuvred her Vespa through the rush hour traffic, guiding us to the parking area she is entitled to as a landlord. She took us to her modern new flat in one of the smaller apartment buildings by the coast. Along the way, she showed us a stone sea wall which used to serve its purpose in the past, but is now dozens of metres from the sea.

The inhabitants of the town – often called Little Venice, even though it is actually a lot older than Venice – used to be very closely connected with the towns on the Slovenian coast, so much so that their Slovenian neighbours used the local name Čožani for them. They have always been known as skilled fishermen and boat makers. They would occasionally infiltrate our side of the bay and would constantly get involved in disputes. Even nowadays, their fishing fleet is unbelievably numerous, especially for someone who comes from an area where fishing is sadly dying out.

The next day, we took a boat to Venice and we were especially interested in seeing the famous lagoon in front of the town with its fishermen's wooden pile dwellings that impressed us so much in the film. The water is so shallow in many places that it makes large areas easily walkable. It felt as though I was looking into the past – what I saw on my cruise was similar to what the adventurers in the fifth century experienced as they sailed into the Venice Lagoon for the first time and chose it as their home. The first Venetians came from Aquileia, which is a town similar to Chioggia (Clodia, Cluza, Clugia, etc.) in that it was established, according to a legend, at some point in the distant past (1185 BC according to Virgil) by Trojan refugees after they had been defeated by the Greek heroes who burned down their city. These refugees were Clodius and his friend Aeneas (Rome), the Trojan prince Antenor (Padua) and Aquilius (Aquileia).

Sixteen centuries later, after the incursion of Attila into the mighty Aquileia, its inhabitants scattered all around the bay and also made it to Piran, Izola and Koper. It would be interesting to study these connections between the towns from Chioggia to Piran – they were probably bound by family and friendly ties in the beginning, just like with the Trojan refugees a good millennium and a half earlier.

Passing the mysteriously sinister islet of Poveglia, where the Venetians would send anyone not welcome in the city, ranging from the infected to the more recent mental patients, we finally arrived in Venice after a two-hour journey.

We found a nice spot on *Riva degli Schiavoni* and gazed into the shimmering, golden reflections of the dreams of Venice's fathers on the emerald water, gently curled by the breeze of the southern wind.

Our Sottomarina apartment was in a house where most units were holiday lets. And since we were in the middle of the Labour Day holidays, the boisterous youths decided to have some fun and hid and mixed up all the slippers, shoes and sandals in the hallway at night. Most of the footwear was then recovered in the morning, only Sanja's favourite Teva sandals, which have seen so much of the world, were gone for good.

Were they only trying to remind us of all the times throughout history when unforeseen events would instantaneously topple the old, only for the future to come up with a new story, possibly even more beautiful than the previous one?

THE SOLAR CYCLE IS COMPLETE AND
ANOTHER SUMMER IS UPON US ...

TAMARA

In spring, before I even started thinking about the upcoming summer and my new guests, I was surprised to receive a message from a friend. He needs an apartment for his French friend and colleague. Would it be okay?

Of course, come! You are welcome!

Alex is a master of subtly detecting energies. Ever since I have had serious medical issues, he got into the habit of checking my energy field every time we meet. He likes to surprise me during everyday conversation by throwing in casual remarks that remind me of certain spiritual shortcomings or lack of focus on my path.

His friend Tamara is also a medium and an intuitive healer. We talk a lot about their work, experiences and sensations.

It happens sometimes that all of us can witness scenes from a certain parallel time and space, but these events are sporadic and we have no control over them, which is why we usually dismiss them as insignificant; however, some manage to hone this ability through years of training into a controlled activity, while a fortunate few are already born with this talent.

They came to the coast because Alex wants to visit some of his friends who need his help, leaving

Tamara and I to our own devices during the day. We travel across Istria, exploring old hillforts and other traces of the *ancients* that abound on this peninsula. Tamara comes from a land which is home to the world-renowned stone alignments in Carnac, with similar ones also located in Menec, Kermario and elsewhere, so it is not surprising that she has a special affinity for them.

On the last day, I invite her to the magical environment of the Istarske Toplice Health Spa Resort near Motovun. I like bathing in the healing water with the distinct smell of sulphur which makes the skin so nice and soft, and I like the pilgrimage trail that leads to the top of a nearby cliff where you find the ruins of the Church of St. Stephen. There are remains of a prehistoric settlement in the vicinity which suggests that the spa was most probably used long before antiquity.

Anyway – the place feels touched by the spirit of ancestors, which always fills me with gratitude that I am able to walk these paths and enjoy the wonderful views, just like so many others had done before me. We stick to my regular routine: bathing first, followed by a hike to the top of the cliff. In clear weather, nice views open up towards Buzet with Mount Učka in the background, and to the right, behind the endless Motovun Forest to the little town of Motovun, you can sometimes just make out the glimmer of a thin line of the sea in the distance.

Tamara closes her eyes and stops in her tracks. *I see a group of girls dressed in white, they are climbing up in a ceremonial procession towards the top.* She opens her eyes, *This is where a shrine used to be, dedicated to a goddess,* she says with conviction.

I admire the ease with which she travels between worlds and glides along the timeline, her switches between the opaque and transparent worlds seem as intuitive as breathing.

We wait at the top, in silence and in tune with the magic of the place, for the sun to slowly slump below the horizon, painting the sky scarlet – as if a dragon had swung its tail before retiring to its cave, leaving the world to enjoy the still of the night.

The next day, it is time for us to say goodbye as well.

Next time, we will visit Monkodonja, a prototype for all urban settlements in Istria – like a young Mycenae, or maybe Troy? I am really looking forward to this as I hold Tamara's hand between my palms.

BEN 2

Dear Maja, last summer in your house and your pleasant garden was wonderful. This year, I would like to show Piran to my friend Veronica. Unfortunately, my son is busy working and will not be able to come with us.

I am looking forward to seeing you!

Ben?!!!

I takes a few minutes of searching my memory. Ben?

The man who proposed to his future wife in this town decades ago? How lovely!

I cannot wait to see what the summer will bring this time around!

Ben enters the garden enthusiastically and spins around to quickly take it all in.

Oh, my dear mystical little house, here I am again!

My daughter calls it Villa Villekulla from Pippi Longstocking, I add with a smile.

We are old friends at this point and we have relaxed conversations in the evenings. Even with Veronica, it feels as though I have known her for ages. She spent her childhood in India and Nepal and her descriptions of these places are incredibly interesting as they come from a different temporal perspective seen through the eyes of a little girl, a clever observer of her surroundings.

They are avid hikers and they go and see a different place every day – they hike the Sečovlje Salt Pans, explore the Parenzana Trail or swim under the Strunjan Cliffs.

Ben sometimes comes back so sweaty and red in the face that I start to worry. I offer them a ride, but they decline emphatically. This year, they plan only on walking. Next year, maybe ...

One evening, I learn that Ben is practicing andragogy – he is teaching the elderly how they can enrich their lives or find a new purpose. Vigorous, full of excitement and showing a thirst for knowledge not seen in many people decades younger than him, he really is the right man for the job.

When do we really become old?

Is it when the world fails to excite us anymore? When we are no longer able to open up to the beauty of the world?

Are we being dragged down by archaic social patterns that in many places around the world still dictate what we should be doing at a certain stage of our lives?

Maybe it is the family ties which sometimes blind us, causing us to forget that we are still the main protagonists in our own story and not our descendants?

It is nice to meet someone like Ben, brimming with childish curiosity, joy, wisdom, tolerance, courage; he is so charmingly full of life and he is able to share this fullness with others time and again and never run out!

ANA AND PIOTR

The fair-haired middle-aged Poles were overcome with such childlike excitement when they saw the sea that it reminded me of the similar feelings I experienced decades ago when my family and I finally made it to Piran after a long and strenuous drive.

I had countless nightmares of hurtling down the steep Ulica IX. korpusa in a vehicle that had just lost its breaks. Driving down that street always filled me with fear and sickness, and I did not trust the engine of our little white Fiat which became the guardian of our lives. However, going down that street also meant that we had finally made it and the terror I had to go through was the price you had to pay for all the fun and joy that followed during the long summer holidays.

Ana puts on her tight red swimsuit that accentuates the soft lines of her body – the body that ignites so much love and passion inside of Piotr.

He admires the soft contours of her face, covered by a lock of curly hair on one side, as they walk through the fields hand in hand. She can feel his eyes on her and she raises her head, causing him to look away quickly.

Should I get down on my knee? He ponders frantically.

Did you get those notes on Renaissance literature in Italy? Ana asks, unknowingly postponing the infatuated boy's proposal once again.

Should I prepare something to eat or should we go swimming first? Ana summons him back into reality.

Let's go for a swim.

He watches the swaying of her hips as she walks towards the water, still so very lustful. He loves her gently and faithfully. He loves those nights when they sit in the homeliness of the living room, in front of the fireplace, each with their own pile of essays that need to be graded. The family dinners with their two sons, family discussions late into the night.

The next day, I prepare a garden hose to water the plants.

Please, may I? he begs, so cute, like a little child. He takes great care of the plants over the next few days, fixes little things around the house and even gets up earlier than usual to hose down the space in front of the front door before it is occupied by delivery carts and bathers.

Everything is done very professionally, as if it were his job.

And what do you do? I ask, returning the question they asked me earlier.

We are university professors. Ana is at the Department of English and I am a historian.

I am surprised by the answer, but now I understand why he likes gardening so much – it is a change.

Every night after dinner, prepared by Ana, they open a bottle of wine and talk softly, leaning in towards each other long into the night until they run out of wine. I am amazed at how much they have to say to each other every single day even after all the decades of being married; how Ana breaks out into laughter every now and then, what a gentleman Piotr is, filling her glass or bringing her a blanket and covering her when she gets cold.

How do they do it, I ask myself. How do they maintain this strong chemistry? Maybe it is because they are humorous, thoughtful and patient with each other? Or is the most important thing the fact that they are equal and witty conversationalists who are genuinely interested in their partner's opinion?

It is such an obvious and trite recipe, but the couples who actually live by it are so rare.

ALICE AND RON

They are hippies in their early middle age. I try to guess what they do for a living. Do they produce music albums? Are they actors?

Alice is petite, slender and tanned, with a face of an angel, while Ron has the look of eternal youth, slightly scruffy, with a small beard of a few days. He is also well aware of how nice he looks.

We occasionally have a quick chat.

Is this your first time here?

Alice tears up.

You know, even though we live in Paris, I was born in Vienna.

My father used to regularly come to Piran. He always said that he would move here after he retires.

He died only three months before his retirement. Lung cancer. I decided to scatter his ashes in the sea on the coast of the town he loved so much.

We will come here every year, on the anniversary. This is the first one. We don't take care of his grave, we don't light candles and we don't put flowers on the marble slab. We prefer to remember him here, in the place that had captivated him.

A small tear automatically runs down her face, a single droplet with the magical power of a great river, washing away the sadness that had been accumulating for the past few days.

Then comes Ron with two cups of camomile tea and I quickly excuse myself so as not to interfere even further with the remembrance of a loved one who has finally gotten his wish to hop along the coast full of colourful houses, maybe as a shiny plankton or maybe a piece of a droplet, sailing on the waves of eternity.

WINDY AND LENA

Ben's joy might just be infectious as it seemingly brought to my house two ladies cut from the same cloth a few months later – Windy and Lena. Two lively travellers and friends are both in their mid-seventies. Windy, who lives in New Zealand, met up with her childhood friend in London so they could travel together to Slovenia.

Upon their arrival, I first gave them a tour of the apartment and then went out to run some errands, convinced that they would want to relax after their strenuous journey. You can imagine my surprise when I came back to find a small group of people in front of the garden gate and hearing Lena's warm laugh booming over everyone's heads. In this short time, they had met a group of boys from England and got into a conversation which kept going long into the night.

The next day, I told them how much I admired their knack for striking up new friendships, saying that most younger women would be envious of their skills.

Actually, none of my guests have ever organised such a lively party.

When it was time to leave, we drove to Ljubljana together. Along the way, I learned that they are also great musicians, no strangers to stages and performing as they

115

used to sing and play in a group together. This could, to a degree, explain their amazing social skills, but still ... hats off, great girls!

I quickly showed them Ljubljana's old town and then we had a farewell sit-down on the river embankment.

Lena and Windy immediately started planning their evening, figuring out which club has good live jazz music, which one of their travel buddies they could invite to tag along.

They are a real inspiration on how to live a full life and to appreciate and be aware of the value of every single moment of our transient life.

About me

I was born on 23 March 1957 in Ljubljana. After finishing my studies at the Faculty of Arts, I got my first job at the Ljubljana City Library and I have been living the past three years of my life in Piran, a small town of creative inspiration.

As soon as my daughter had grown up a bit, we set off on our first travels. First to Egypt, which completely enchanted us with the unfathomable wealth of its ancient culture as with its distinctness, liveliness, chaos and the purity of its people. The spiral of travelling kept growing outwards, taking us to increasingly remote and unknown places where we discovered incredibly heartfelt cultures and the kindness of the locals. They give me endless inspiration to pack up my suitcase and leave to explore the world at every opportunity.

*During my first summer after retiring, my daughter's friend was telling me rather enthusiastically how she travelled across Portugal with the help of the **Airbnb** platform which enables you to find interesting private accommodation.*

Her story got me so excited that I used the platform to put up my ground floor apartment in Piran for let in just a few days.

Soon, the first guests came ... That was the beginning of this experience which has grown into many small stories and, sometimes, friendships as well.

These short stories are just glimpses of passing encounters, written down in the hopes that they would help readers pass the time on their holidays or travels, on the train, or maybe while waiting at the airport. While we wait, let a path open before us towards a new life adventure ...

Maja Sotenšek

AIRBNB STORIES

Illustrated by Miriam Monica
Translated from Slovenian to English by Tine Verbič
Design: Sandra Pohole, k8dizajn.si
Published and Copyright: Maja Sotenšek
Published on demand
Piran, 2021

CIP - Kataložni zapis o publikaciji
Narodna in univerzitetna knjižnica, Ljubljana

821.163.6-32

SOTENŠEK, Maja
   Airbnb stories / Maja Sotenšek ; [illustrated by Miriam Monica ;
translated from Slovenian to English by Tine Verbič]. - Piran :
[author] M. Sotenšek, 2021

ISBN 978-961-07-0464-5
COBISS.SI-ID 57301251